C000171021

ELECTRIC SMOKER COOKBOOK FOR BEGINNERS

Flavorful Electric Smoker Recipes for Cooking Meat, Fish, Vegetables, and Cheese

Christopher Lester

TABLE OF CONTENTS

POULTRY 22

TURKEY 32

PORK 40

LAMB 52

INTRODUCTION

I don't know about you, but summertime has always been special to me. Three months off from school, playing outside all day, and standing around the smoker with my dad and his friends always made me feel like a grownup. In my family, some of our best memories are about sitting at the table while my dad unveiled the prize of his labor — a perfectly smoked brisket, pork butt, chicken, or even a turkey. As I write this book, my parents are still alive, but I will always remember the look of pride in my father's eyes as he placed a perfectly smoked rack of ribs on the dinner table. I can still remember how the meat would just melt in my mouth as the mix of smoke and spices danced on my tongue.

It was later, when I bought my first house and smoker, that I also came to realize the intense competition between men when it comes to smoking food. I like most of my neighbors, but the feeling of besting one on a "smoke-off" is truly a magical moment. My pork ribs with apple/cherry/hickory smoke are legendary in my neighborhood and may have contributed to one of my neighbors' divorce when his wife declared my ribs were better than his. Needless to say, I love to cook, and I love my smoker.

Luckily for us, smoking is no longer just a summertime activity. The ease and relatively "set it and forget it" mentality of electric smoker manufacturers allows us to smoke food all year long. We can do this without having to stand outside all day in the freezing cold of winter to manage the firebox and temperature of a traditional wood-fire smoker.

Smoking our food is now a year-round activity that I enjoy with my wife and kids. With just a few adjustments, smoking in the winter is just as easy as smoking in the summer. Over the years, I have learned a few tips and tricks to using my electric smoker, and I now understand the pride my dad felt when he served a perfectly smoked meal.

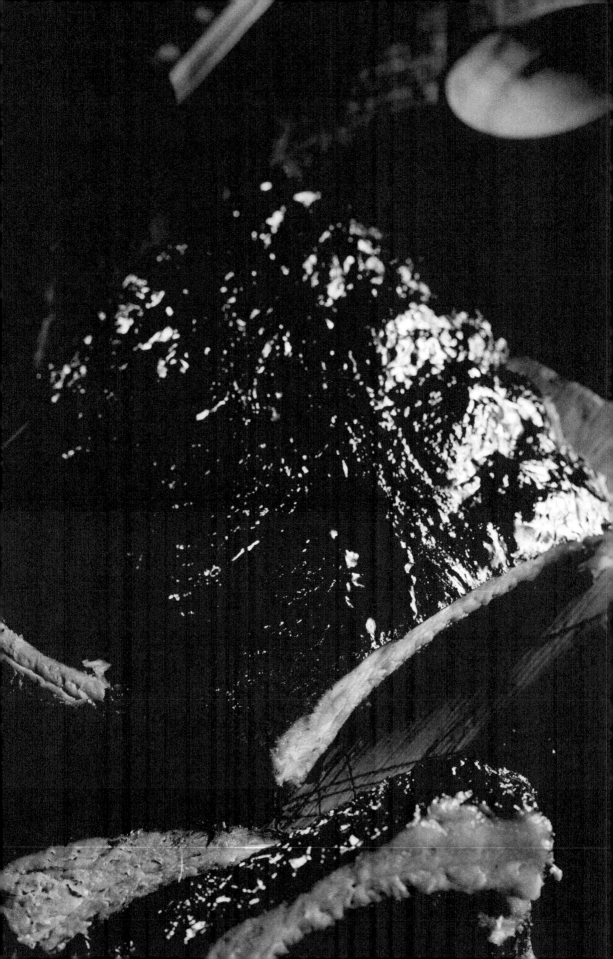

WHAT IS ELECTRIC SMOKING?

We should probably start by talking about what smoking food is. **Smoking is the process of slowly cooking food over a fire.** Wood chunk, chips, or wood pellets are added to give a smoky flavor to whatever you are cooking. This is a lot different from drying meats, vegetables, and fruits. Drying uses a process that requires the moisture of the food to be "brought out" (usually by packing it in salt) before smoking it at a cool temperature; I usually keep it at around 75^0F (25^0C). This process is intended to kill the bacteria so that the meat or fruit can be eaten in its raw state. What I am talking about is called hot smoking. Depending on what I'm smoking, I usually keep the temperature of my smoker between 175 and 250^0F ($80\text{-}120^0C$). This method thoroughly cooks the food while infusing it with smoky flavors. *So, what is electric smoking?*

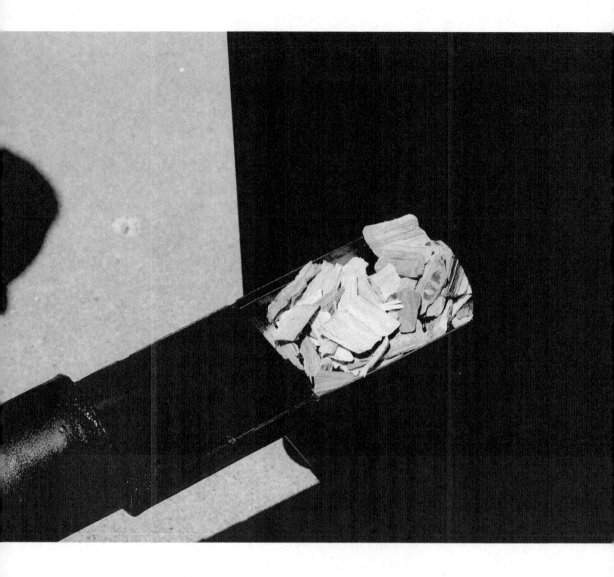

Let me start by telling you what electric smoking is not. Electric smoking is not standing out in the sun all day, fire tongs in hand, singed arm hair, and complaining about the "damn wind ... can't keep the barrel hot" while alternating between drinks of your local microbrew IPA and opening and closing air-ports on your barrel smoker. It also isn't buying bags of pellets only later to play the what-is-it game: "smoker pellets or 'organic' cat litter?" There is a constant battle with a traditional wood-fire smoker to keep the smokers hot enough without getting too hot by managing airflow and fire intensity. Pellet smokers are easier to work, but there may be a risk; pellets are simply sawdust that is heated and pressurized into molds. The pellets are then coated in something to hold the pellet together. While this coating is usually a product of the tree itself, I wonder if it is healthy.

Compared to other forms of smoking food, **electric smokers are the easiest to use and require less attention.**

- You just plug it in
- Set up your hydration method (nobody likes dry meat)
- Add wood chips, set the temperature
- And forget about it until you need to add wood chips

This isn't to say that electric smoking is foolproof; I have turned many a brisket into charred, dried-out chunks of meat that no amount of barbecue sauce can save. You do have to pay attention to your electric smoker, but you at least have some time to finish your beer while it's cold and catch an inning of the MLB game of the day.

Now, traditionally, people seem to have this idea that smoking meat is a summertime ordeal. That kind of thinking might have worked when we were all hunting our food, but we now have grocery stores. Smoking is year-round now. If I want to smoke a brisket, all I need to do is visit the grocery store or the butcher. Smoking is perfect at any time of the year if you want to slow cook your food while infusing it with the goodness of smoke. Smoking in winter is just as easy as smoking in the summer. Both require a little bit of planning.

THE PROCESS OF ELECTRIC SMOKING

While not as simple as a traditional wood-fire smoker and not nearly as complicated as a pellet smoker, electric smokers are an excellent middle ground. An electric smoker doesn't generally take up as much space on the patio, and you don't have to keep it at the far end of the yard, so the house doesn't fill with smoky goodness. Personally, I don't mind the smell in my house. My kids, on the other hand, complain when the smoke alarms go off. Most electric smokers are made up of just a handful of parts. An electric smoker is more like an electric oven that we use outside (don't tell my wife that;

next thing I know, she'll be taking that over too). An electric smoker is just a metallic box with an electric heating element in its bottom and a door and vents built into it. Most are vertical models that allow for the stacking cooking racks, a small bowl for liquid (more about this later), a drip pan, and a wood chip tray.

So, the box (smoke chamber) is just that — a box with a door on it. Most are rectangular, although there are a few that are round. Most are made of a steel or aluminum alloy around a quarter-inch thick with some form of insulation on the inside (usually cement board wall or thick ceramic fiber cloth). You can have one custom-made with thicker walls, but this gets expensive. Just like your oven, your box needs to be sealed reasonably well. The better the seal, the more smoke to work with, and the easier it is to maintain a steady temperature. Make sure you check the welds along the corners, and there should be a tight fit where the door meets the chamber. There should be a small opening in the bottom of the chamber where the cord for the heating element enters it; this should be sealed with a rubber grommet. Many digital models come with thermostats that allow users to set a specific temperature setting, making the process even easier.

The internal construction of your electric smoker is pretty standard. The heating element sits on the bottom of the smoker. On top of that sits the wood chip box. Some models put a water pan next to the chip box,

while others stack it on top. Your drip pan should sit below your heating element. Your cooking racks should be evenly spaced above the water pan. By the way, make sure you use your drip pan properly. If not, the drippings from whatever you are smoking will build up at the bottom of the chamber or will drip into the wood chips, which — trust me on this — will cause a fire.

Now that the smoker is all put together, how it works is easy to understand. It is basically a convection system. The heating element heats the air inside the chamber and heats the wood chips to their smoke point — not hot enough to combust and catch fire, but enough to create smoke. As the hot air and smoke circulate through the chamber, it slowly brings the food to temperature while the smoke from the chips soaks into the meat. Forgive me if there is a bit of drool on the page; *thinking about smoking makes my mouth water.*

DIFFERENT BRANDS OF ELECTRIC SMOKERS

There are hundreds of different brands of smokers of varying price ranges. One thing to remember — price doesn't always mean a well-built, long-lasting smoker. Proper maintenance and care of your smoker will extend its lifespan and provide years of great food. The constant thing that every electric smoker has is either digital or analog controls. Digital temperature controls allow you to set the specific temperature you want to cook your food; you don't need as much heat or time to smoke cheese as you do a turkey. Analog controls consist of a thermostat and vents that are opened or closed to adjust the temperature.

The smokers that I've listed here are ones that I have experience with or have received excellent reviews on Amazon.com, electricsmokerers.com, smokedbbqsource.com, or theburningbrisket.com.

MASTERBUILT

Masterbuilt smokers are one of the most popular brands in the United States. They have been making outdoor cooking equipment for over 45 years and continuously work to improve their products. Masterbuilt offers a wide variety of both digital and analog smokers of different sizes to meet your needs. Masterbuilt did patent their chip-loading system that lets users add chips to the smoker without opening the door. This is beneficial because having the sideload means that less heat and smoke are released when adding chips than when you have to open the main door. They also offer a ton of options, like built-in meat probe thermometers and Bluetooth control. With Bluetooth, you never have to get off the couch except to put your food in and take it out; you won't miss that last-second field goal anymore.

CHAR-BROIL

Another wildly popular electric smoker manufacturer is Char-Broil. Like Masterbuilt, Char-Broil offers several electric smokers readily available in most national home and garden chains (e.g., Home Depot, Lowes, and Walmart). Most of the Char-Broil line of smokers have a glass insert in the door. While this doesn't help or hurt the smoking process, it does let you watch your food cook while drinking a beer. I find this helpful when the kids get particularly testy or when the mother-in-law drops by for a visit.

BRADLEY TECHNOLOGIES

Bradleys are, I think, the Cadillac of electric smokers. Available in both analog and digital models, these things can be used for both hot and cold smoke, and it works as an oven and dehydrator as well. What makes this brand different is that they use a separate side box for chips (they use a unique product called a Bisquette) attached to the main chamber, each with its own individually controlled heating element. This means that you can control the amount of smoke and the temperature of the main chamber to vary the smoke flavor in your foods.

BASIC MAINTENANCE

No matter what brand of electric smoker you buy, you need to maintain it. This is true no matter whether you purchased the $99 special at Walmart or ordered a $1,400 custom smoker; the key to great tasting food and longevity is proper cleaning and maintenance. We must do our best to fight our male instincts and save the user manual; manufacturers always give cleaning instructions. If you're like me and you "lost it," you can usually find a manual online.

Some manufacturers suggest that you clean your smoker after every use. Others say you should clean it after every three to five uses. I wouldn't put it off more than **five uses before cleaning** as the soot from the smoke and grease from the food buildup can be dangerous and affect the efficiency of the smoker.

Remember, as you use your smoker, the interior will get dark in color. This is normal and needed; it prevents rust and can help in the smoking process. We're not talking about a deep cleanse; you should focus on **removing food bits and grease**. I recommend you clean your smoker when it is still warm and before the grease hardens. Remove the racks, drip pan, wood box, and water bowl, then gently scrape off the excess grease and food bits. Wipe everything down with mild soap and water and put your smoker back together. You can let it sit open for about an hour, and the excess water and soapsuds will eventually evaporate (this method works better in the summer months). I prefer to take the faster route. Once you've wiped out the excess water and soap, close the smoker up and crank it up on high, grab a beer, and let it burn for 30 minutes. This ensures that the water evaporates entirely and whatever little soap bubbles that are left burn off.

BENEFITS OF SMOKING IN ELECTRIC SMOKERS

Periodically, I am asked, "Why should I buy an electric smoker?" I have a couple of answers for this. The first reason is that electric smokers are perfect for people just starting to learn how to cook with smoke. Smoking isn't rocket science, but there are some subtle nuances that we pick up along the way.

Because electric smokers maintain constant heat, you can smoke things for extended periods without worrying about the temperature of your smoker. Think about it — you can put your pork butt in it before bed, and it will be ready to shred when you wake up in the morning. I don't know about you, but to me, this means that I can have dinner in the smoker while I go to work during the day.

Second, let's talk about time. **Electric smokers will save you time** because most follow the "set it and forget it" mentality. We all lead hectic lives. Wives, kids, work — the list of our duties never ends. Now, you don't have to miss your kids' peewee football game on Saturday; just set your smoker and forget about it. Most models have timers on them now, and if you get one with an adjustable temperature gauge, the risk of turning your chicken into charcoal is relatively small. With all of that extra time on your hands, you can experiment with different rubs and sauces, which, in my house, comes with a mix of excitement and fear.

Electric smokers are, oddly, more environmentally conscious and are safer to use than traditional wood-fire smokers. I am not going to lie; I have both an electric and wood-fire smoker. To date, I have never had an electric smoker catch on fire. On the other hand, I almost burned down the back fence and came close to a visit from the fire department with my wood-fire smoker. Further, common knowledge teaches us that electricity is much cleaner to use than burning propane, charcoal, or wood. Smoke particulates are harmful to the environment and the health of others. Remember, electric smokers don't burn the wood; rather, it heats the wood to its smoke point without combustion.

KINDS OF WOOD CHIPS

No matter what brand of electric smoker Obviously, if you're going to smoke food, you need to know what wood to use. The most important thing to avoid is resin-rich woods, like pine or cedar. These tend to coat the food in a strange film and make for a strong, bitter taste. Cedar planks may be good for grilling fish in a regular barbecue, but not for a smoker. Most smoker enthusiasts will tell you to stick with hardwoods, and I agree.

Oak and hickory are the most popular woods for beginners and the most common in general. Oak tends to give a medium flavor without being overpowering. It is excellent on red meats — beef, lamb, and sausages.

Hickory is a bit sweeter and hearty, but it can easily make meat bitter if you use too much. Hickory is good with pork, poultry, and most red meats.

Maple is a great choice for game fowl, pork, and poultry. It gives a subtler smoky flavor with a light sweetness. Fruit woods, such as **cherry, apple, and pear**, are amazing for chicken, turkey, and pork. I have used a mix of cherry and hickory when I smoke trout. Fruit woods leave a sweeter smoke taste with just a hint of fruit flavor.

For smoking fish, I like to use **alder wood**. It is a particularly delicate flavor that pairs well with fish, like salmon or trout.

ADDITIONAL EQUIPMENT

Not all electric smokers are sold with everything that you will need. For example, Masterbuilt includes meat thermometer probes, but Char-Broil and Bradley smokers don't. For safety and comfort purposes, you need to pick up a few extra things.

- *A waterproof cover:* You just spent your hard-earned money to buy an electric smoker, so protect it and extend its life by shielding it from the weather when you're not using it.

- *Wireless meat thermometer:* Not all smokers come with meat thermometers. Trust me on this; there is nothing worse than having to break out the chainsaw to slice your brisket. Similarly, there is nothing as disheartening as pulling out your chicken, only to find that it is still raw at the bone. A wireless meat thermometer allows you to monitor the temperature of the smoker or meat without having to open the door (letting out heat) or leaving the couch as they come with a readout device or connect via Bluetooth to your smartphone.

- *Gloves:* These need to be heat-resistant and washable. Years ago, my mother-in-law bought me a pair of heat-resistant neopropoline Darth Vader gloves. These have saved me from burning my hands-on countless occasions as I add wood chips or move the food around while it's smoking.

- *Metal scraper/putty knife:* You need this to clean your smoker. Pro tip: Clean your smoker while it is warm. The gloves you bought earlier will prevent you from burning your hands.

- *Fire extinguisher:* Electric smokers are considerably safer than wood-fire smokers, but accidents happen. If you have a buildup of grease or you're smoking particularly fatty foods (like bacon), there is a slight chance the heating element can set the fat drops on the fire.

- *Spare parts:* Things happen, and parts break. Having a spare heating element, chip tray, or drip can save you from a smoking disaster.

- *Beer (or the beverage of your choice):* Smoking food isn't done quickly; it is a process that requires time and patience. If you're going to spend time waiting for your smoker to do its job, you might as well stay well hydrated doing it.

TROUBLESHOOTING

You dropped a bunch of cash on an electric smoker, and now something is wrong: the food may have a chemical taste, your smoker isn't heating up, or perhaps, the smoke is too thick or too thin. While you should always follow the manufacturer's recommendations, here are a few helpful hints.

1. Food has a chemical taste.

This usually happens because some cleaning residue is left from the factory or the last time you cleaned it. Regardless of whether it is right out of the box or you've just cleaned it, you need to season your smoker. To season your smoker, set the temperature to 275°F and let it sit for about 2.5 hours. For the last 30 minutes, put about a cup of wood chip in the chip tray and let it go. After 3 hours, turn the smoker off and let it cool.

2. Your electric smoker won't start, or it keeps tripping the breaker.

The first thing you should do is to make sure it is securely plugged in. If it is plugged in, then the problem is either your heating element or the electrical socket itself. If you are using a GFCI breaker, chances are your smoking is drawing more power than the breaker can handle; try a new electrical socket. If it isn't the breaker, it is probably the heating element. You can clean your heating element with dish soap and water. *Pro tip:* Use a propane torch to burn off any moisture or buildup on the heating element. If that doesn't work, be glad you bought a spare heating element "just in case."

3. The smoke is too thick/thin.

If the smoke is too thick, you probably need to clean your smoker. Your smoker is probably burning the creosote buildup, which isn't healthy to eat and is a fire risk. If your smoke is too thin, this isn't the fault of your smoker; it's either the wood or the user. Make sure you are using dried, cured wood, and avoid using softwoods, like pine or fir. Make sure you have adequate ventilation of your smoker by opening the dampers on the bottom.

EASY HERB SMOKED CHICKEN

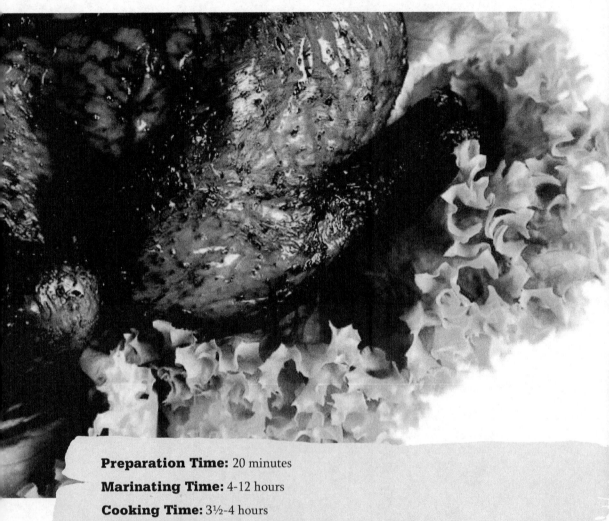

Preparation Time: 20 minutes

Marinating Time: 4-12 hours

Cooking Time: 3½-4 hours

Serves: 6 - 8

Preferred Wood: Hickory (a robust, slow-burning wood with a sweet flavor)

Nutrition Guidelines (per serving)

Calories 426; Total Fat 10.5g; Saturated Fat 4g; Cholesterol 200mg; Sodium 178mg; Total Carbohydrate 6.3g; Dietary Fiber 0g; Total Sugars 6.4g; Protein 72.7g, Vitamin D 2mcg, Calcium 33mg, Iron 2mg, Potassium 468mg

For the brine:

8 black peppercorns (whole)

1 cup (250 g) kosher salt

4 whole cloves

4 sprigs of fresh rosemary

A few fresh sage leaves

A few sprigs thyme

1 cup (240 g) brown sugar

For the meat:

8 small sprigs rosemary

2 Tbsp. garlic powder

2 whole chickens

(about 4-5 lb (2-2½ kg) each)

2 Tbsp. kosher salt

1 Tbsp. fresh black pepper

2 Tbsp. sweet smoked paprika

2 Tbsp. butter

1. Brine the chicken. Fill a medium-sized saucepan about ⅔ of the way full with water, and bring up to medium heat.

2. Add salt, sugar, pepper, and rosemary to the lightly simmering water.

3. Crush thyme, black peppercorns, sage, and cloves and add them to the saucepan.

4. Gently simmer until the sugar and salt have dissolved and all ingredients are well combined.

5. Place the chickens in a large container and add the brine mixture over the top, along with enough cold water to cover. Place the container in the fridge and leave to sit for up to twelve hours, but no less than four hours.

6. (This is our standard technique for brining poultry and other meats; it will be referred to throughout this guide.)

For the meat:

7. Preheat your smoker to 250-275⁰F (120-135⁰C). While preheating, add your hickory wood chips to the loading tube.

8. Once your chickens have brined sufficiently, you have the option to remove the backbone, which will enable them to lay flat and cook more evenly. Place the chickens with the spine facing up and the drumsticks towards you. Taking a pair of strong kitchen scissors, snip all the way along one side of the backbone. Repeat on the other side of the backbone, using your hands, remove it from the chicken. Do not cut through the center of the backbone itself. When the backbone is removed, turn the chicken over and press it out flat. This technique is known as spatchcocking.

9. Season generously with salt and pepper.

10. Massage the paprika, garlic powder, and rosemary over the skin of the birds.

11. Gently slide your fingers underneath the skin along the breast of the bird, being careful not to break the skin. Once you have created a natural opening under the lining of the skin, divide your butter up and add it to the opening. Massage the top of the skin so that the butter spreads evenly across the breast.

12. Add the rosemary sprigs to the underside of the skin.

13. Add a little vegetable oil to the chicken's skin, along with a last pinch of salt.

14. Smoke for around 3½ to 4 hours until the internal temperature of the meat reaches 165⁰F (75⁰C).

BEER CAN CHICKEN

Preparation Time: about 15-20 minutes

Marinating Time: about 4 hours in a liquid brine

Cooking Time: 2-3 hours

Serves: 8-10

Preferred Wood: Cherry (imparts a mild, fruity, sweet flavor with a subtle smokiness)

Nutrition Guidelines (per serving)

Calories 867; Total Fat 38g; Saturated Fat 9.3g; Cholesterol 362mg; Sodium 1800mg; Total Carbohydrate 8.2g; Dietary Fiber 0.3g; Total Sugars 2.9g; Protein 116.3g, Vitamin D 0mcg, Calcium 68mg, Iron 5mg, Potassium 1000mg

For the rub:

¼ tsp. dried sage

1 Tbsp. brown sugar

1½ tsp. garlic powder

1½ tsp. salt

⅔ tsp. pepper

¾ tsp. smoked paprika

½ tsp. dry mustard

¼ tsp. cayenne pepper

For the meat:

2 whole pre-brined chickens
(about 3-4 lb. (1½-2 kg) each)

1 cup (250 ml) mayonnaise

1. Preheat your smoker to 225-275^{0}F (110-135^{0}C) and add your cherry wood to the loading tube.

2. Create your beer-can stand setup. You will need two beer cans (if you prefer, you can leave some beer inside the can, but they should only be about halfway full). You can drink the other half! Ease the cavity of the chickens over the top of the cans and use the legs of the bird to support its weight.

3. Combine the rub ingredients and mayonnaise and apply to the outside of the chicken.

4. Place the beer cans (with the chickens on top) inside a foil pan or a metal sheet inside the smoker, and smoke for around 2-3 hours until their internal temperature reaches 165^{0}F (75^{0}C).

SMOKED MAPLE-GLAZED CHICKEN WITH BBQ RUB

Preparation Time: about 10-15 minutes

Marinating Time: about 4 hours

Cooking Time: approximately 3 hours

Serves: 3-5

Preferred Wood: Pecan (a robust, nutty, and rich-flavored wood)

Nutrition Guidelines (per serving)

Calories 765; Total Fat 27.4g; Saturated Fat 7.5g; Cholesterol 323mg; Sodium 2875mg; Total Carbohydrate 17.7g; Dietary Fiber 1g; Total Sugars 13g; Protein 106.3g, Vitamin D 0mcg, Calcium 88mg, Iron 5mg, Potassium 1003mg

For the rub:

1½ tsp. garlic powder

1 Tbsp. brown sugar

½ Tbsp. dry mustard

½ tsp. black pepper

¾ tsp. sweet paprika

1½ tsp. salt

1½ tsp. onion powder

1 tsp. smoked paprika

For the meat:

1 whole pre-brined chicken
(approximately 4 lb. (1.8 kg))

¼ cup (85 g) maple syrup

1. Preheat your smoker to around 250⁰F (120⁰C) and add your pecan wood to the loading tube.

2. Brush the chicken all over with the maple syrup, making sure to get into all the cracks and crevices. Reserve about 2 tablespoons of maple syrup.

3. Combine all of the dry rub ingredients in a bowl (reserving about 1 tablespoon of the rub mixture for later), and sprinkle this mixture over the top, sides, back, and inside of the bird. Make sure every part is thoroughly coated.

4. Place the chicken on the smoking rack breast side downwards.

5. Smoke the bird for approximately 3 hours, glazing with more of the maple syrup combined with any leftover rub at intervals. Remember that not all smokers cook at the same temperature. Be sure to use a meat probe or thermometer to determine when your bird is done – its internal temperature should be 165⁰F (75⁰C).

BACON-WRAPPED SMOKED CHICKEN BREASTS

Preparation Time: about 10-15 minutes

Marinating Time: only if you choose to brine

Cooking Time: 3-3½ hours

Serves: 4-5

Preferred Wood: Hickory (hickory chips add to the bacon's natural smoky flavor)

Nutrition Guidelines (per serving)

Calories 1141; Total Fat 72g; Saturated Fat 22.9g; Cholesterol 315mg; Sodium 3626mg; Total Carbohydrate 11.9g; Dietary Fiber 0.2g; Total Sugars 9.4g; Protein 104.3g, Vitamin D 0mcg, Calcium 52mg, Iron 4mg, Potassium 1257mg

For the rub:

2 lb. (1 kg) chicken breasts (this will be approximately four or five breasts, depending on their size)

1 tsp. smoked paprika

1 heaped tsp. chili powder

1½ lb. (700 g) thick-cut bacon slices

⅓ cup (80 g) brown sugar

½ tsp. salt

½ tsp. black pepper

One small pinch of cayenne pepper

1. Preheat your electric smoker to around 225^{0}F (110^{0}C) and add your hickory chips to the loading tube.

2. Remove the fat from each of the breasts with a sharp knife.

3. Season the breasts on every side with salt and pepper.

4. Wrap a strip of bacon around each breast, making sure to tuck in the loose ends. Sprinkle a little pepper on the bacon (it doesn't need salt as the bacon is naturally salty). This will stop the breast from drying out when it is inside the smoker. Secure the ends of each bacon rasher with a toothpick to stop it from coming loose.

5. Stir together the sugar, chili powder, cayenne pepper, and paprika in a small bowl.

6. Sprinkle the mixture over the bacon-wrapped breasts.

7. Place the breasts on the cooking rack inside the smoker and smoke them at 225^{0}F (110^{0}C) for approximately 3 to 3½ hours, depending on their thickness.

8. Once done, heat up a frying pan and give them a quick fry to crisp up the bacon layer.

GEORGIA-STYLE SMOKED PULLED CHICKEN

Preparation Time: 10 minutes

Marinating Time: 4 hours

Cooking Time: 2 hours

Serves: 4

Preferred Wood: Hickory

Nutrition Guidelines (per serving)

Calories 740; Total Fat 28.3g; Saturated Fat 7.9g; Cholesterol 334mg; Sodium 326mg; Total Carbohydrate 6.4g; Dietary Fiber 1.9g; Total Sugars 3.1g; Protein 109.3g, Vitamin D 0mcg, Calcium 124mg, Iron 7mg, Potassium 982mg

For the rub
(makes ¼ cup of mixture):

1 Tbsp. dried thyme

1 Tbsp. black pepper

1 crushed bay leaf

2 Tbsp. dried sage

1 Tbsp. dried rosemary

1 Tbsp. dried oregano

1 Tbsp. dried parsley

1 Tbsp. dried basil

1 Tbsp. sugar

For the meat:

3.3 lb. (1½ kg) whole chicken, pre-brined

Salt and pepper for seasoning

1. Preheat your smoker to around 275^{0}F (135^{0}C) and add the hickory wood chips to the loading tube while it preheats.

2. Spatchcock the chicken, as described in "Easy Herb Smoked Chicken."

3. Season the chicken and coat the portions thoroughly with a portion of the rub.

4. Smoke for around 2 hours at 275^{0}F (135^{0}C) until the internal temperature of the meat is 165^{0}F (75^{0}C).

5. Transfer the portions to a hot griddle and sear the skin on high heat for a few minutes until crispy.

6. Once cooled, pull the meat apart with your fingers.

TURKEY WITH CAJUN-STYLE RUB

Preparation Time: 10-15 minutes

Marinating Time: leave to chill for 12-24 hours

Cooking Time: 5-6 hours

Serves: 8-10

Preferred Wood: Hickory

Nutrition Guidelines (per serving)

Calories 935; Total Fat 48.7g; Saturated Fat 18.1g; Cholesterol 368mg; Sodium 3563mg; Total Carbohydrate 4.7g; Dietary Fiber 0.7g; Total Sugars 3.3g; Protein 103.6g, Vitamin D 6mcg, Calcium 14mg, Iron 0mg, Potassium 50mg

½ cup (113 g) softened butter

2 tsp. smoked paprika

1 small onion

2 tsp. of cayenne pepper

2 tsp. oregano

1 whole lemon

1 bay leaf

3 Tbsp. light brown sugar

1 whole turkey (12-14 lb. / 5½-6½ kg)

3 Tbsp. coarse sea salt

1 tsp. garlic powder

1. Preheat your electric smoker to 225^{0}F (110^{0}C) and add the hickory wood chips to the loading tube.

2. Blend the salt, sugar, paprika, oregano, cayenne pepper, and garlic in a small bowl and set to the side. Scoop 1 tablespoon into a separate bowl for later.

3. Dry the turkey with paper towels.

4. Smear the inside of the turkey's cavity with the Cajun rub and coat the outside, being sure to massage it into the skin.

5. Place the turkey in a plastic bag or container and leave it in the fridge for at least 12 to 24 hours.

6. Infuse the remaining tablespoons of Cajun rub into the softened butter. Ease your fingers underneath the skin without breaking it so that you can place the butter along the breast bone. Place the butter at intervals on the breast. Massage the top of the skin so that the butter is evenly spread underneath the skin. Apply any remaining butter to the top of the turkey.

7. Cut the lemon and onion in half and place inside the cavity of the turkey, along with the bay leaf.

8. Secure the legs of the turkey using strong twine and leave to rest for 30 minutes.

9. Place the turkey inside the smoker with the breast pointing upwards. Smoke the turkey for 5 to 6 hours or until the internal temperature reaches just slightly less than 165^{0}F (75^{0}C). The bird will continue to cook while it rests.

10. Let it stand for about 20 to 25 minutes to reabsorb its juices. Cover with foil to protect it from drying out.

SMOKED
TURKEY WINGS

Preparation Time: 5 minutes

Marinating Time: not necessary in this recipe

Cooking Time: around 2 hours

Serves: 3

Preferred Wood: Mesquite (a lighter and brighter flavor than hickory smoke, popular in Southwestern-style cooking)

Nutrition Guidelines (per serving)

Calories 1037; Total Fat 64.9g; Saturated Fat 0g; Cholesterol 357mg; Sodium 2017mg; Total Carbohydrate 4.9g; Dietary Fiber 0.4g; Total Sugars 2g; Protein 107g, Vitamin D 0mcg, Calcium 16mg, Iron 7mg, Potassium 23mg

1 cup (250 ml) premade BBQ sauce

½ tsp. dried oregano

1 tsp. garlic powder

1 tsp. ground mustard

¼ tsp. dried and crushed rosemary

¼ tsp. dried thyme

⅔ Tbsp. kosher salt

½ tsp. dried parsley

3 large turkey wings (approximately 3 lb. / 1.5 kg)

1. Preheat the electric smoker to 275⁰F (135⁰C) and add your mesquite wood chips to the loading tube.

2. Incorporate the dry ingredients together in a bowl.

3. Remove the tip of each turkey wing with a sharp knife.

4. Toss the wings in the spice and herb mixture.

5. Smoke the wings for around 2 hours at 275⁰F (135⁰C), until the internal temperature of the meat is around 165 or 170⁰F (75⁰C). Baste every 20 minutes or so with the BBQ sauce in order to keep the meat moist.

CHERRY GLAZED SMOKED TURKEY

Preparation Time: 20 minutes

Marinating Time: not necessary in this recipe

Cooking Time: 6 hours (+ 15 minutes to rest)

Serves: 10-15

Preferred Wood: Cherry or hickory

Nutrition Guidelines (per serving)

Calories 790; Total Fat 27.7g; Saturated Fat 11.9g; Cholesterol 302mg; Sodium 329mg; Total Carbohydrate 21.4g; Dietary Fiber 0.2g; Total Sugars 17.1g; Protein 107.6g, Vitamin D 6mcg, Calcium 18mg, Iron 37mg, Potassium 1115mg

For the rub
(makes 6 cups, so adjust as needed):

1 lb. (450 g) brown sugar   3 Tbsp. cumin

3 Tbsp. pepper   1¼ (340 g) cups salt

3 Tbsp. garlic powder

2 Tbsp. oregano

⅓ cup paprika

⅓ cup cinnamon

⅓ cup chili powder

For the glaze:

1 Tbsp. butter

2 sprigs rosemary

1¼ cup (320 g) cherry preserve

¼ cup (60 ml) balsamic vinegar

2 cloves garlic

For the meat:

1 whole turkey (12-14 lb. / 5½-6½ kg)

2 Tbsp. rub

½ cup (113 g) softened butter

For the glaze:

1. Melt butter over medium-low heat and incorporate the garlic and rosemary. Heat it until you can smell the garlic beginning to cook, and then add the balsamic vinegar.

2. Reduce for about 2 minutes, and then slowly add the cherry preserve to the mixture. Mix gently until the ingredients are incorporated.

3. Remove from the heat and leave to cool.

For the meat:

4. Preheat your smoker to around 250⁰F (120⁰C) and add your preferred choice of wood to the loading tube. Cherry works well with the cherry glaze of the turkey, but hickory wood also adds a traditional earthiness and a sweet, smoky flavor.

5. Clean the inside of the bird, removing any leftover giblets, etc.

6. Combine dry rub ingredients and coat the turkey thoroughly.

7. Massage the softened butter into the breast and the thickest parts of the bird to stop them from drying out.

8. Place the turkey in a foil pan and smoke for approximately two hours until the skin has taken on a golden color.

9. Cover the turkey with foil, and smoke for a further 5 hours. Test the internal temperature, making sure that it reaches 150⁰F (65⁰C).

10. After around 5 hours, glaze the bird with the cherry mixture and check the internal temperature. Once it reaches 165⁰F (75⁰C), remove it from the smoker and tent with foil to rest for around 30-40 minutes.

PEACHY MESQUITE SMOKED TURKEY

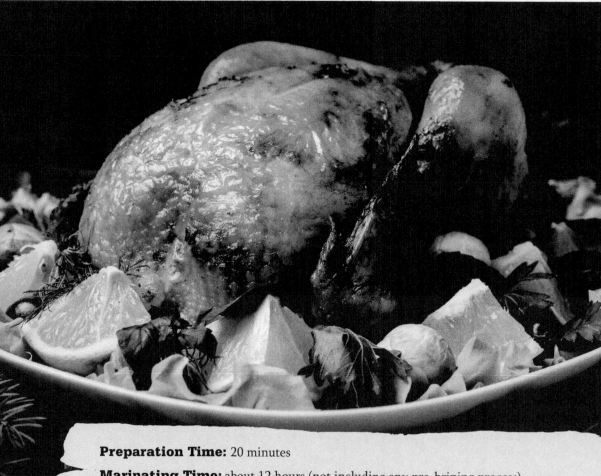

Preparation Time: 20 minutes

Marinating Time: about 12 hours (not including any pre-brining process)

Cooking Time: 7-8 hours (30 minutes per pound)

Serves: 10-15

Preferred Wood: Mesquite

Nutrition Guidelines (per serving)

Calories 689; Total Fat 29.5g; Saturated Fat 9g; Cholesterol 250mg; Sodium 1707mg; Total Carbohydrate 18g; Dietary Fiber 1.3g; Total Sugars 12.1g; Protein 75.9g, Vitamin D 0mcg, Calcium 16mg, Iron 1mg, Potassium 107mg

For the rub:

3 Tbsp. dark brown sugar

1 tsp. ground cumin

2 tsp. dry mustard

1 tsp. coarse black pepper

2 Tbsp. paprika

1 tsp. granulated onion powder

1 Tbsp. garlic powder

1 Tbsp. coarse sea salt

2 tsp. chili powder

2 tsp. Korean-style chili flakes

For the glaze:

The juice of two oranges

¾ cup (200 g) of peach jam or marmalade

3 Tbsp. of rice wine vinegar or any white wine vinegar

1 jalapeno pepper, finely chopped

1 Tbsp. of Dijon mustard

1 Tbsp. fresh ginger minced

For the meat:

1 whole pre-brined, cleaned turkey (12-16 lb. / 5½-7 kg)

2 lemons or oranges cut in half (optional)

1 large red onion cut in half

For the rub:

1. Combine all the ingredients in a bowl and set aside.

For the meat:

2. Lay the turkey inside a large foil pan and pat dry.

3. Massage the rub onto the surface and into the cavity of the bird so that it is completely covered in the mixture.

4. Cover the turkey and allow it to chill in the fridge for about 12 hours.

5. Combine all of the ingredients for the glaze in a small saucepan, stirring over low heat for about 5 to 10 minutes, and set aside.

6. Remove the turkey from the fridge, truss (tie) the legs with twine, and insert the oranges, lemons, and onion inside the turkey's cavity.

7. Set the turkey aside to rest while your smoker preheats to a temperature of around 225⁰F (110⁰C). Add the mesquite wood chips to the loading tube.

8. Smoke the turkey for around 7-8 hours, basting twice in the last hour of cooking using the peach glaze.

DELICIOUSLY SMOKY BOSTON PORK BUTT

Preparation Time: about 10 minutes

Marinating Time: not necessary in this recipe

Cooking Time: 8-9 hours (1 hour per pound)

Serves: 8-12

Preferred Wood: Apple (a wood with very mild, sweet, and subtle fruity flavor)

Nutrition Guidelines (per serving)

Calories 497; Total Fat 16.8g; Saturated Fat 5.6g; Cholesterol 230mg; Sodium 626mg; Total Carbohydrate 3.7g; Dietary Fiber 0.3g; Total Sugars 3.1g; Protein 78g, Vitamin D 0mcg, Calcium 51mg, Iron 3mg, Potassium 963mg

For the rub:

½ tsp. cayenne pepper

2 tsp. onion powder

1 tsp. dry yellow mustard

1 Tbsp. coarse sea salt

2 tsp. smoked paprika

1 tsp. ground black pepper

¼ cup (60 g) brown sugar

2 tsp. roasted garlic powder

For the meat:

Around 6-8 lb. (3-3½ kg) of pork butt with the fat trimmed

1. Preheat the smoker to around 225^{0}F (110^{0}C) and add apple wood chips to the loading tube.

2. Combine the dry rub ingredients and rub them onto the pork.

3. If it has been in the fridge, leave it to rest for about 20 minutes in a foil pan to get up to room temperature.

4. Smoke for approximately 8-9 hours until the core temperature of the meat reaches 190^{0}F (90^{0}C).

5. The pork butt should be meltingly tender at this point. Allow it to cool, and use a fork to pull the meat apart. Serve the pork with your favorite hot sauces or a sweet BBQ sauce. This meat goes well on sandwiches, pizzas, inside wraps, etc.

ZINGY BBQ RUB SMOKED PORK CHOPS

Preparation Time: 10 minutes

Marinating Time: about 4 hours in a brining solution

Cooking Time: 1 hour

Serves: 4

Preferred Wood: Apple

Nutrition Guidelines (per serving)

Calories 361; Total Fat 23.9g; Saturated Fat 8g; Cholesterol 69mg; Sodium 74mg; Total Carbohydrate 19g; Dietary Fiber 1.3g; Total Sugars 16.7g; Protein 18.6g, Vitamin D 0mcg, Calcium 54mg, Iron 2mg, Potassium 379mg

For the BBQ rub:

¼ tsp. cayenne pepper

1 Tbsp. garlic powder

1 Tbsp. smoked paprika

1 tsp. dry mustard powder

1 Tbsp. onion powder

1 Tbsp. black pepper

½ cup (120 g) brown sugar

2 Tbsp. sweet paprika

1 Tbsp. kosher salt

For the meat:

4 thick-cut bone-in pork chops (about 1½ inches thick)

½ tsp. ground allspice

2 tsp. whole peppercorns

8 cups (2 l) of water

3 Tbsp. white sugar

¼ cup (60 g) kosher salt or sea salt

2 tsp. crushed fennel seeds

1 bay leaf

2 cloves garlic

1 Tbsp. olive oil

3 Tbsp. of the rub mixture

1. Brine the chops. Lay them in a flat container and cover them with about a cup of boiling water. Ensure that the container can fit in the refrigerator easily.

2. Gently stir in the sugar and salt into the water until they have both dissolved.

3. Add the fennel, allspice, bay leaf, garlic, peppercorns, and a few sprigs of thyme to the water and leave it to infuse.

4. Pour about 7 cups of cold water over the mixture and place the chops in the fridge, covered, for about 7 to 24 hours.

Cooking the chops:

5. Preheat the smoker to around 250⁰F (120⁰C), adding your apple wood chips to the loading tube as you do so.

6. Remove the chops from the brine and pat them dry with a paper towel.

7. Heat up a large skillet to medium-high heat and add about a tablespoon of vegetable oil to it.

8. Rub the BBQ rub into the chops.

9. Sear the chops on both sides briefly (3 or 4 minutes per side, depending on the chop's thickness).

10. Once done, allow the chops to rest for about 5 minutes. At this point, your pork chops should not be cooked through completely.

11. Smoke the pork chops for about an hour or until the internal temperature of the meat reads 145⁰F (65⁰C).

DELECTABLE SMOKED PORCHETTA WITH HERBS

Preparation Time: 30 minutes

Marinating Time: there's no marinating in this recipe, but it does require 12 hours of air-drying

Cooking Time: around 3½ hours

Serves: 10

Preferred Wood: Apple

Nutrition Guidelines (per serving)

Calories 590; Total Fat 35g; Saturated Fat 12.6g; Cholesterol 174mg; Sodium 1522mg; Total Carbohydrate 0.7g; Dietary Fiber 0.5g; Total Sugars 0.2g; Protein 59.9g, Vitamin D 0mcg, Calcium 18mg, Iron 1mg, Potassium 8mg

5 lb. (2 1/3 kg) pork belly, skin on

2 lb. (1 kg) boneless center-cut pork loin with the fat trimmed

3 Tbsp. fennel seeds

2 Tbsp. fresh sage leaves, crushed

2 Tbsp. fresh rosemary, crushed

3 cloves garlic, peeled and minced

Zest of one lemon

Zest of one orange

2 tsp. of sea salt

1½ tsp. of black pepper

1 tsp. of red pepper flakes

1. Place a wire rack inside a foil pan and lay the pork belly and loin on top. Place in the fridge and allow to chill for about 12 hours. Remove from the fridge 30 minutes before cooking.

2. Preheat the smoker to around 235⁰F (110⁰C) and add your apple wood chips to the loading tube.

3. In a small bowl, incorporate the fennel, sage, rosemary, garlic, salt and pepper, orange and lemon zest, and red pepper flakes.

4. Pat the pork belly dry with paper towels. With a stanley knife or another sharp knife, score the top of the belly at intervals. Flip the belly over and coat well with the herb and spice mixture.

5. Roll the belly around the loin until the two edges meet. Tie tightly with kitchen twine.

6. Place the now rolled pork belly and loin on a rack over a foil pan (to catch the drippings).

7. Place the pan inside the smoker and smoke for around 3 to 3½ hours, replacing the wood as and where needed.

ELECTRIFYING SMOKED BABY BACK PORK RIBS

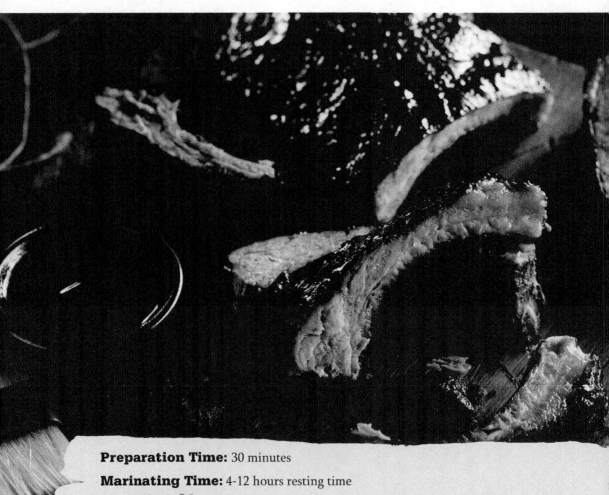

Preparation Time: 30 minutes

Marinating Time: 4-12 hours resting time

Cooking Time: 1½ hours

Serves: 6-10

Preferred Wood: Hickory

Nutrition Guidelines (per serving)

Calories 636; Total Fat 33.9g; Saturated Fat 13.6g; Cholesterol 210mg; Sodium 196mg; Total Carbohydrate 7.4g; Dietary Fiber 0.1g; Total Sugars 6.6g; Protein 71.7g, Vitamin D 0mcg, Calcium 35mg, Iron 7mg, Potassium 1089mg

For the rub:

1 tsp. cayenne pepper

1½ tsp. garlic powder

1½ tsp. dried oregano

1½ tsp. of dry mustard

2 Tbsp. dark brown sugar

1 tsp. freshly ground black pepper

¾ cup (200 g) apple juice

2 tsp. paprika

2 Tbsp. kosher salt

1 tsp. dried thyme

1 tsp. onion powder

For the meat:

2 racks of baby back ribs (3 lb. / 1½ kg each) with the membrane removed

1. Mix the rub ingredients well.

2. Rub the mixture all over the ribs and cover with plastic wrap. Leave them to sit in the fridge for a couple of hours or overnight.

3. When it's time to start cooking, preheat the smoker to around 250^{0}F (120^{0}C) and add hickory wood chips to the loading tube.

4. In a bowl, combine the apple juice, leftover rub, salt, and ¾ cup of water.

5. Wrap each set of ribs in heavy-duty foil.

6. Smoke the ribs for one hour with the lid closed, occasionally turning to maintain an even distribution of heat. Increase cooking time if needed, judging by the internal temperature of the meat. You're looking for an internal temperature of around 145^{0}F (65^{0}C).

7. Continually baste the ribs with the remaining rub and apple juice mixture for another 30 minutes.

8. Once the ribs are done, remove the foil and allow them to rest for about 10 minutes.

9. Baste the ribs with what is left of the basting sauce. Char the ribs on a hot grill if needed.

10. Cut the ribs into even slices and serve warm.

TANGY TEXAS-STYLE SMOKED PULLED PORK NACHOS

Preparation Time: 30 minutes

Marinating Time: not necessary in this recipe

Cooking Time: 12-13 hours

Serves: 8

Preferred Wood: Apple

Nutrition Guidelines (per serving)

Calories 670; Total Fat 49.8g; Saturated Fat 19.2g; Cholesterol 188mg; Sodium 245mg; Total Carbohydrate 4.7g; Dietary Fiber 0g; Total Sugars 4.5g; Protein 48.3g, Vitamin D 2mcg, Calcium 184mg, Iron 3mg, Potassium 641mg

For the rub:

1 tsp. garlic powder

1½ tsp. chipotle seasoning

1 tsp. cayenne pepper

½ tsp. ground black pepper

1 tsp. chili powder

¼ cup (60 g) light brown sugar

1 tsp. onion powder

1 Tbsp. smoked paprika

1 Tbsp. salt

For the meat:

1 bone-in pork shoulder (approximately 3 lb. / 1½ kg)

A couple of tablespoons of olive oil

A big bag of nachos or corn tortillas

An assortment of cheeses, such as Monterey jack, cheddar, American cheese, etc.

1. Preheat the smoker to around 275°F (135°C) and add pre-soaked apple wood pieces to the loading tube.

2. Combine all the rub ingredients in a small bowl.

3. Coat the pork shoulder liberally in olive oil, then massage the rub blend into the meat.

4. Lay the pork on a wire rack over a foil pan (to catch the drippings), and place in the smoker.

5. Smoke the pork shoulder for around 5 hours, then remove to wrap in heavy-duty tinfoil.

6. Place back in the smoker and smoke for another 8 hours.

7. Once done, let it rest on a plate covered with tinfoil for about 30 minutes.

8. After it has cooled, use a fork or other sharp implement to pull the meat apart.

9. Preheat the oven to around 350°F (175°C).

10. Place your nachos, the meat, and your cheese of choice in layers on top of a greased sheet pan. Place in the preheated oven for around 10 minutes until the cheese has melted. Leave to cool for about 10 minutes.

11. Serve with guacamole, salsa, cotija cheese, sour cream, or your choice of desired toppings and sauces.

SWEET, SMOKY, AND STICKY HONEY-BAKED HAM

Preparation Time: 1 hour

Marinating Time: about 45 minutes to rest initially, unless brining

Cooking Time: 4 hours

Serves: 15-16

Preferred Wood: Apple

Nutrition Guidelines (per serving)

Calories 507; Total Fat 24.4g; Saturated Fat 8.2g; Cholesterol 162mg; Sodium 3699mg; Total Carbohydrate 22.4g; Dietary Fiber 3.7g; Total Sugars 10.5g; Protein 47.3g, Vitamin D 0mcg, Calcium 79mg, Iron 3mg, Potassium 845mg

¼ cup (60 g) pineapple juice

½ cups (170 g) maple syrup

10-16 lb. (4½-7 kg) bone-in pre-baked ham (shoulder, butt, or shank)

½ cups (225 g) light brown sugar

2 Tbsp. hot English mustard

1. Remove the pre-baked ham from the packaging and pat dry with paper towels. Place the ham on a wire rack set over a metal sheet or tray and leave it for about an hour to get up to room temperature.

2. Preheat the smoker to around 240-250⁰F (115 - 120⁰C) and add the apple wood chips to the loading tube.

3. Place the foil pan, with the ham, in it on the lower section of the smoker. Open the top ventilation hatch.

4. Smoke the ham until it reaches an internal temperature of 130⁰F (55⁰C) (this should take about 1½ to 2½ hours). Continually check the ham, using a meat probe or a thermometer, to see if it is at the right temperature. Replace water and chips as needed.

5. Place a small saucepan on the stove and turn it to low heat. Add the sugar, juice, mustard, and syrup, and allow to simmer for around 5 to 10 minutes. You'll know it's ready when it coats the back of a spoon. Wait for the glaze to cool and place in a small dish.

6. Lightly brush the ham with the glaze when you remove the first time (about 1½ to 2½ hours) and return it to the smoker for another 1½ hours (if it is a smaller ham, you may want to remove it sooner).

7. Remove the ham from the smoker and cover with foil. Leave it to stand for about 15 minutes to avoid it drying out.

STYLISHLY SMOKED GREEK LEG OF LAMB

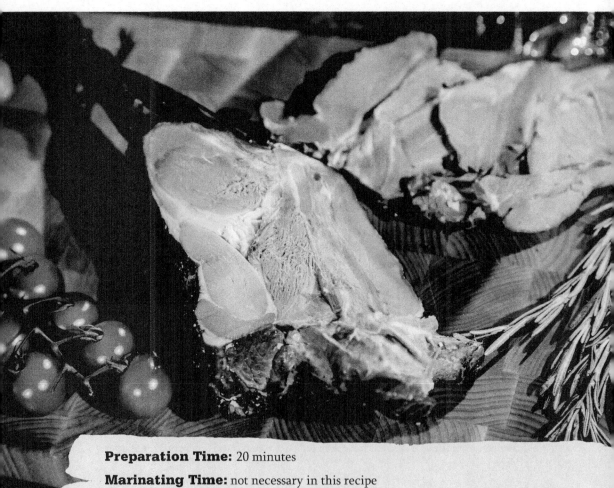

Preparation Time: 20 minutes

Marinating Time: not necessary in this recipe

Cooking Time: 3½ to 4 hours depending on the size of the cut and the leg

Serves: 6

Preferred Wood: Hickory

Nutrition Guidelines (per serving)

Calories 427; Total Fat 14.9g; Saturated Fat 0.7g; Cholesterol 0mg; Sodium 2327mg; Total Carbohydrate 2.4g; Dietary Fiber 1g; Total Sugars 0.1g; Protein 67.3g, Vitamin D 0mcg, Calcium 37mg, Iron 1mg, Potassium 48mg

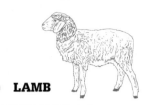

1 tsp. dried thyme

2 Tbsp. olive oil

2 Tbsp. kosher salt

1 Tbsp. fresh black pepper

1 leg of lamb (2-2½ lb. / 1 kg)

4 garlic cloves peeled and crushed

2 Tbsp. oregano

1. Trim any excess fat off the lamb, taking care not to remove too much of the meat. Try to ensure that the meat is an even shape so that it cooks evenly. You can use a piece of butcher's string to tie up the lamb so that it sits evenly on the cooking surface.

2. Preheat the smoker to 250°F (120°C) and add the hickory wood pieces to the loading tube.

3. Combine the garlic, oil, salt and pepper, and herbs in a small dish.

4. Rub the lamb all over with the mixture and cover it with a layer of plastic wrap. Place the lamb in a dish in the fridge for about an hour.

5. After resting for 10 minutes, smoke the lamb for around 3½ hours, testing the internal temperature frequently. It will be done when it reaches around 145°F (65°C).

TEXAN-STYLE OAK-SMOKED LAMB LEG

Preparation Time: around 30 minutes

Marinating Time: 12 hours resting time overnight

Cooking Time: around 3 hours

Serves: 6-8

Preferred Wood: Oak (an all-round versatile wood with a medium smokiness and a more pronounced flavor than apple or cherry)

Nutrition Guidelines (per serving)

Calories 491; Total Fat 19.3g; Saturated Fat 6.7g; Cholesterol 225mg; Sodium 1512mg; Total Carbohydrate 4.4g; Dietary Fiber 1.3g; Total Sugars 2.6g; Protein 71.1g, Vitamin D 0mcg, Calcium 55mg, Iron 7mg, Potassium 923mg

For the rub:

1 Tbsp. yellow mustard seed

2 Tbsp. smoked paprika

1 Tbsp. coriander seed

1 Tbsp. cumin seed

1½ Tbsp. kosher salt

1 Tbsp. Korean chili flakes

1½ tsp. chipotle seasoning

2 Tbsp. brown sugar

For the meat:

1 leg of lamb bone-in (approximately 5-7 lb. / 2-3 kg)

1. In a small pan over medium heat, gently toast the coriander, mustard, and cumin seeds until slightly smoking.

2. Grind up the seeds in a pestle and mortar. Incorporate them into the rest of the dry ingredients in a bowl.

3. Vigorously rub the dry rub into the leg of lamb so that it is completely coated. Cover the leg of lamb with a piece of plastic wrap and place it in a container in the fridge overnight.

4. The next day, bring the leg of lamb out and let it rest for about 15 or 20 minutes to get up to room temperature.

5. Preheat your smoker to 250°F (120°C) and add your oak wood chips to the loading tube.

6. Smoke the lamb for about 3 hours or until the internal temperature of the meat reaches around 145°F (65°C).

7. Remove the lamb from the smoker and rest it on a tray, covered loosely with foil, for about 10 to 15 minutes before serving.

AMAZING AMERICAN-STYLI MESQUITE SMOKED LAMB CHOPS

Preparation Time: 15 minutes

Marinating Time: an hour for resting and chilling

Cooking Time: 50 minutes to 1 hour

Serves: 5-6

Preferred Wood: Mesquite

Nutrition Guidelines (per serving)

Calories 351; Total Fat 16.9g; Saturated Fat 5g; Cholesterol 150mg; Sodium 127mg; Total Carbohydrate 0.1g; Dietary Fiber 0.1g; Total Sugars 0g; Protein 46.8g, Vitamin D 0mcg, Calcium 23mg, Iron 4mg, Potassium 562mg

1 tsp. coarse kosher salt

½ tsp. freshly ground black pepper

2 Tbsp. olive oil

1 Tbsp. balsamic vinegar

1 rack of lamb trimmed and divided into single sliced chops

1. Preheat your electric smoker to around 225°F (110°C) and add the pre-soaked mesquite chips to the loading tube.

2. In a small bowl, blend the olive oil, salt and pepper, and balsamic vinegar, and evenly coat the lamb chops with this mixture.

3. Lay the lamb chops in a flat dish and cover with plastic wrap. Place the dish in the fridge and leave to chill for about 1 hour. When the chops come out of the fridge, set them aside to rest for about 15-20 minutes to get up to room temperature. This ensures more even cooking.

4. Place the chops on a wire rack set over a foil pan and smoke for about 45 minutes to an hour, or until the internal temperature of the meat is around 140°F (60°C).

SMOKED LAMB LEG WITH A PICTURE-PERFECT HERBED CRUST

Preparation Time: 30 minutes

Marinating Time: 4-6 hours

Cooking Time: 2-2½ hours

Serves: 8-10

Preferred Wood: Hickory

Nutrition Guidelines (per serving)

Calories 416; Total Fat 11.1g; Saturated Fat 1g; Cholesterol 4mg; Sodium 901mg; Total Carbohydrate 11.1g; Dietary Fiber 1g; Total Sugars 1.2g; Protein 64g, Vitamin D 0mcg, Calcium 86mg, Iron 1mg, Potassium 72mg

LAMB

For the marinade:

1 Tbsp. Dijon mustard

1 Tbsp. coarse kosher salt

1 tsp. minced garlic

½ freshly ground black pepper

1 Tbsp. olive oil

1 Tbsp. crushed rosemary leaves

For the meat:

1 6-8 lb. (3-3½ kg) lamb leg bone-in

15-20 garlic cloves, halved

¼ cup (60 g) Dijon mustard

For the herb crust:

1 Tbsp. salt

1 cup (120 g) breadcrumbs (Japanese panko breadcrumbs work the best here, but any dry breadcrumbs will do)

½ tsp. ground black pepper

½ cup (50 g) grated parmesan cheese

¾ (60 g) cup of your choice of mixed spices

1. Trim the fat from the leg of lamb if it has not already been trimmed.

2. Make several slits into the meat about an inch apart across the leg. Insert whole garlic cloves into these slits and push them down into the meat.

3. Place all of the marinade ingredients in a food processor except the oil. Blend the ingredients and add the olive oil slowly as the ingredients are being blended. You should end up with a thick, paste-like consistency.

4. Wrap the leg in plastic wrap and leave to marinate in a container in the fridge for four to six hours.

5. Preheat the smoker to around 225⁰F (110⁰C) and add your pre-soaked hickory chips to the loading tube.

6. Allow the leg to rest at room temperature for about 15-20 minutes before cooking.

7. Combine the crust ingredients inside a small dish. Set aside.

8. Remove the leg from the marinade and, using a pastry brush, coat lightly with the Dijon mustard.

9. Roll the leg of lamb in the crust ingredients so that it is evenly coated on all sides. The mustard should help the herb crust ingredients stick to the outside of the meat.

10. Place the leg on a wire rack set over a tray and smoke the leg for about 2 hours or until the internal temperature of the meat reads 140-145⁰F (60⁰C).

11. Remove the leg carefully from the smoker and cover it loosely with tin foil, allowing it to rest for about 20 minutes before serving.

SUMPTUOUSLY SMOKED PULLED LAMB SHOULDER

Preparation Time: 20 minutes

Marinating Time: not necessary in this recipe

Cooking Time: 8-9 hours

Serves: 5-7

Preferred Wood: Pecan

Nutrition Guidelines (per serving)

Calories 558; Total Fat 21.7g; Saturated Fat 7.6g; Cholesterol 257mg; Sodium 219mg; Total Carbohydrate 5g; Dietary Fiber 1.4g; Total Sugars 2.2g; Protein 81.2g, Vitamin D 0mcg, Calcium 60mg, Iron 8mg, Potassium 1041mg

1 Tbsp. hot English mustard

1½ Tbsp. light brown sugar

1 approximately 5 lb. (2-2½ kg) lamb shoulder

2 Tbsp. coarse kosher salt

1 Tbsp. fresh mustard seeds

4 cloves garlic lightly crushed

2 Tbsp. sweet paprika

1½ Tbsp. ground black pepper

1 Tbsp. crushed or roughly chopped rosemary leaves

1. Preheat the smoker to around 225^{0}F (110^{0}C) and add your pre-soaked pecan wood chips to the loading tube.

2. Trim the lamb for any excess sinew or fat.

3. Incorporate the garlic, rosemary, mustard seeds, sugar, salt and pepper, and paprika together in a small container.

4. Paint the mustard all over the shoulder using a pastry brush.

5. Place the lamb on the indirect heat inside the smoker and smoke for around 8-9 hours or until the internal temperature of the meat is around 200^{0}F (95^{0}C).

6. Remove the lamb and leave to rest for around 30 minutes, tented with foil.

SMOKED BRISKET

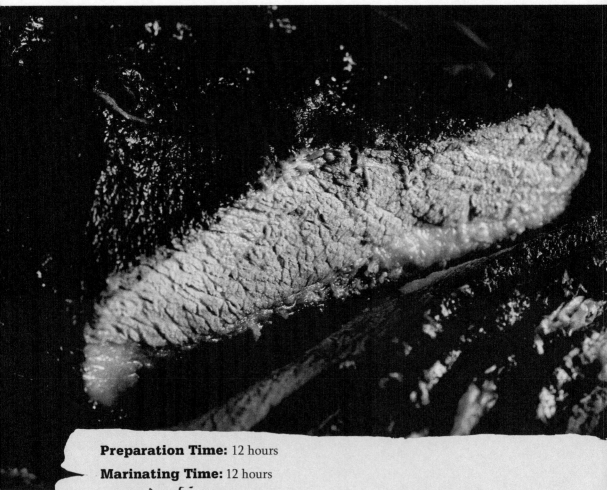

Preparation Time: 12 hours

Marinating Time: 12 hours

Cooking Time: 14 hours

Serves: 12

Preferred Wood: Cherry

Nutrition Guidelines (per serving)

Calories 732; Total Fat 23.7g; Saturated Fat 8.9g; Cholesterol 335mg; Sodium 831mg; Total Carbohydrate 8.3g; Dietary Fiber 0.9g; Total Sugars 6.4g; Protein 114.2g, Vitamin D 0mcg, Calcium 19mg, Iron 71mg, Potassium 1582mg

For the rub:

1 Tbsp. garlic powder

½ cup (125 g) brown sugar

1 Tbsp. smoked paprika

1 Tbsp. freshly ground black pepper

2 Tbsp. sweet paprika

1 Tbsp. kosher salt

1 Tbsp. onion powder

¼ tsp. cayenne pepper

1 tsp. mustard powder

For the meat:

1 brisket, 10-13 lb. / 4½-6 kg (flat cut, point or packer)

1 cup (130 g) of the BBQ spice rub (recipe above)

1. Trim the brisket of any excess fat and sinew.

2. Combine the rub ingredients in a small bowl.

3. Completely cover the brisket with the dry rub, ensuring that it is evenly coated.

4. Place in a covered container inside the fridge for about 12 hours.

5. Preheat your smoker to around 250ºF (120ºC) and add your cherry wood chips to the loading tube.

6. Smoke the brisket for around 4-5 hours, ensuring that the temperature gets up to around 170ºF (75ºC).

7. Remove the brisket from the smoker and cover it completely with tin foil.

8. Place the brisket back into the smoker and smoke it for a further 9-10 hours, ensuring that it gets up to the internal temperature of 200ºF (95ºC).

9. Once the brisket has finished smoking, allow it to rest for around 10 minutes covered, and another 5 minutes uncovered before serving.

SMOKED PRIME RIB OF BEEF

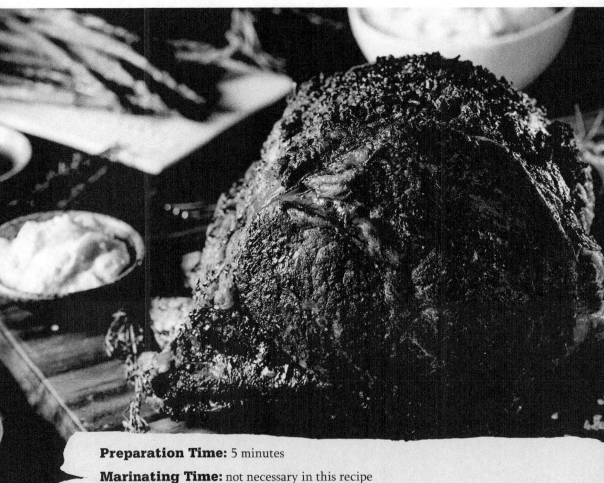

Preparation Time: 5 minutes

Marinating Time: not necessary in this recipe

Cooking Time: 5½ to 6 hours (35 minutes per pound)

Serves: 8-10

Preferred Wood: Mixture of oak and cherry

Nutrition Guidelines (per serving)

Calories 1116; Total Fat 83.3g; Saturated Fat 32.7g; Cholesterol 269mg; Sodium 2520mg; Total Carbohydrate 8.7g; Dietary Fiber 1.2g; Total Sugars 0.6g; Protein 77.1g, Vitamin D 0mcg, Calcium 47mg, Iron 1mg, Potassium 59mg

1 10 lb. (4½ kg) prime rib roast tied and with all the bones removed

½ cup (125 g) horseradish mustard

2 Tbsp. horseradish sauce

4 cloves garlic minced

Coarse salt and black pepper

1. Preheat your smoker to around 225⁰F (110⁰C) and add in the mixture of cherry and oak wood chips to the loading tube. You can add any ratio of the woods, depending on which flavor you want more of.

2. Trim the excess fat from the prime rib, along with any and all sinew. Leave about ¼ inch of fat on top of the roast.

3. Blend the mustard, garlic, and horseradish in a small bowl. Completely cover the roast in the mixture, and season it all over with salt and pepper to taste.

4. Place the prime rib inside the smoker and smoke until the internal temperature of the meat reaches around 120⁰F (50⁰C) for rare doneness. This will take about 5 hours, depending on the thickness of your cut.

5. Place the roast on a cutting board and rest it, covered with foil, for 20 minutes.

6. Turn your grill or smoker up to the maximum heat and place the prime rib back on the hot side of the grill for about 15-20 minutes. This will impart further smoked flavor to the ribs.

7. Place the roast on a serving platter and allow to rest for a further 30 minutes before serving.

SMOKED BACON-WRAPPED FILET MIGNON

Preparation Time: 20 minutes

Marinating Time: 2 hours

Cooking Time: 1 hour

Serves: 8-10

Preferred Wood: Oak

Nutrition Guidelines (per serving)

Calories 697; Total Fat 35.3g; Saturated Fat 12.7g; Cholesterol 254mg; Sodium 632mg; Total Carbohydrate 4.3g; Dietary Fiber 0.7g; Total Sugars 1.8g; Protein 85.4g, Vitamin D 0mcg, Calcium 29mg, Iron 1mg, Potassium 166mg

For the rub
(makes enough for 6 portions):

Kosher salt

2 Tbsp. garlic powder

1 Tbsp. dried cumin

Freshly ground black pepper

2 Tbsp. dried oregano

2 Tbsp. onion powder

1 Tbsp. light brown sugar

For the meat:

6 lb. (3 kg) filet mignon steaks (1 per person)

Kosher salt

1 slice of thin cut bacon per steak

Olive oil

1. Place the steaks on a wire rack set over a tray. Using the ratio of ½ teaspoon of coarse kosher salt per steak, salt the tops of each steak evenly and place the tray in the fridge for about 2 hours.

2. Place a strip of bacon on a cutting board. Standing the steak up vertically, wrap the bacon around the outer edge of the steak and secure it in place using a toothpick. Do the same for all the other steaks.

3. Combine the dry rub ingredients inside a small bowl. Apply the rub liberally on all sides of the steaks.

4. Preheat the smoker to around 225^0F (110^0C) and add the oak wood chips to the loading tube.

5. Place the steaks directly over the non-direct heating section of the smoker and smoke for 1 hour, or until the internal temperature of the meat reaches 130^0F / 55^0C (if you like it medium-rare).

6. Let the steaks rest for approximately 10 minutes.

7. Heat up a skillet to medium and add approximately 1 tablespoon of vegetable oil. Gently sizzle the steaks' sides so that the bacon takes on a crispy texture, which will really enhance the flavor of the steaks themselves.

8. As an additional step, you can quickly flash fry or sear the finished smoked steaks in a hot skillet to add another layer of caramelized flavor. This should only take a few minutes, maybe 5 or 10.

SMOKED BEEF HAMBURGER PATTIES

Preparation Time: 12 minutes

Marinating Time: not necessary in this recipe

Cooking Time: 1 hour

Serves: 7

Preferred Wood: Hickory

Nutrition Guidelines (per serving)

Calories 222; Total Fat 9.3g; Saturated Fat 4g; Cholesterol 30mg; Sodium 491mg; Total Carbohydrate 23.8g; Dietary Fiber 1.3g; Total Sugars 5.2g; Protein 10.8g, Vitamin D 0mcg, Calcium 163mg, Iron 2mg, Potassium 172mg

2 lb. (1 kg) ground chuck

1 Tbsp. kosher salt

1½ tsp. cracked black pepper

Additional: Hamburger buns, American cheese slices, lettuce, tomato, and dill pickle slices.

1. Preheat the smoker to around 225^{0}F (110^{0}C) and add the hickory chips to the loading tube.

2. Form the ground chuck into balls about 5-6 (150 g) ounces each. Flatten each of them out evenly into identically shaped burgers. Liberally season the burgers on both sides with salt and pepper.

3. Place the patties on the cooking racks inside the smoker and smoke them for about 1-1½ hours or until they have an internal temperature of around 160^{0}F (70^{0}C).

4. Before the burgers are completely cooked through, add a slice of cheese to the top of each inside the smoker and leave to continue cooking so the cheese melts.

SMOKED RIBEYE STEAKS WITH A ZESTY TWIST

Preparation Time: about 10 minutes

Marinating Time: not necessary in this recipe

Cooking Time: 1 hour

Serves: 4

Preferred Wood: Cherry

Nutrition Guidelines (per serving)

Calories 322; Total Fat 25g; Saturated Fat 11.2g; Cholesterol 68mg; Sodium 58mg; Total Carbohydrate 4g; Dietary Fiber 0.5g; Total Sugars 1.8g; Protein 18.5g, Vitamin D 0mcg, Calcium 25mg, Iron 2mg, Potassium 368mg

4 ribeye steaks
1½ tsp. chopped dill
1 Tbsp. garlic powder
1 Tbsp. olive oil
Kosher salt and black pepper
1 Tbsp. onion powder
Zest of one orange

1. Preheat the smoker to 225°F (110°C) and add your pre-soaked cherry wood chips to the loading tube, along with a cup of water to the drip tray.

2. Place the steaks on a board. Season them well with salt, pepper, onion powder, and garlic powder.

3. Mix the olive oil, dill, and zest in a small bowl, and, using a pastry brush, apply it to the steaks.

4. Leave the steaks to rest for about 15 minutes to get up to room temperature.

5. Smoke the steaks for approximately one hour, replacing the wood and water as necessary.

6. Check the internal temperatures of the steaks often. For rare, it needs to be at 120°F (50°C). For medium-rare, it needs to be at 125°F (55°C), and for medium-well, it needs to be at 145°F (65°C).

7. Once the steaks are done, allow them to rest for about 10 minutes before serving. If desired, the steaks can be seared in a hot skillet to improve the color and give them an added flavor layer.

CAJUN-STYLE SMOKED BUTTERFLIED SHRIMP

Preparation Time: 15 minutes

Marinating Time: 2 hours

Cooking Time: 20 minutes

Serves: 6-9

Preferred Wood: Alder (a very delicately flavored, slightly sweet wood, perfect for the subtle flavors of seafood)

Nutrition Guidelines (per serving)

Calories 156; Total Fat 5.6g; Saturated Fat 0.8g; Cholesterol 311mg; Sodium 1755mg; Total Carbohydrate 0g; Dietary Fiber 0g; Total Sugars 2.8g; Protein 27g, Vitamin D 0mcg, Calcium 162mg, Iron 1mg, Potassium 0mg

For the rub (makes around 12 Tbsp. (170 g) of mixture):

2 Tbsp. mixed herbs

1 tsp. chipotle seasoning

2 Tbsp. coarse kosher salt

1 Tbsp. cayenne pepper

2 Tbsp. garlic powder

1 Tbsp. dried thyme

1 Tbsp. onion powder

1 Tbsp. black pepper

For the shrimp:

3 lb. (1½ kg) of jumbo shrimp, cleaned and peeled

¼ cup (33 g) of olive oil

1. Butterfly the shrimp. Split them down the middle using a sharp knife, but do not cut them in half.

2. Place the shrimp inside a Ziploc container or bag along with the oil and ¼ cup of the rub mixture. Shake the bag thoroughly so that all of the ingredients are combined.

3. Leave the bag in the fridge for about 2 hours so the shrimp can pick up all the marinade flavors.

4. When the shrimp comes out of the fridge, start preheating the smoker to around 225°F (110°C). Add your alder wood to the loading tube.

5. Flatten out the butterflied shrimp. Place them inside the smoker inside a foil pan, so they are evenly spread out. Close the lid of the smoker fully.

6. Smoke the shrimp for around 15-20 minutes.

SIMPLY STUNNING SMOKED SALMON

Preparation Time: 15 minutes for making the brine

Marinating Time: 8 hours brining time

Cooking Time: 12 hours

Serves: 8-10

Preferred Wood: Alder or mesquite

Nutrition Guidelines (per serving)

Calories 565; Total Fat 22.6g; Saturated Fat 3.2g; Cholesterol 160mg; Sodium 7705mg; Total Carbohydrate 20.8g; Dietary Fiber 0.1g; Total Sugars 19.3g; Protein 71g, Vitamin D 0mcg, Calcium 137mg, Iron 2mg, Potassium 1416mg

2 cups dark soy sauce

½ cup (125 g) coarse kosher or sea salt (don't use ordinary table salt here, as it will cure the fish and make it dry)

1½ tsp. minced garlic

1 Tbsp. minced ginger

8-10 lb. (3½-4½ kg) salmon, filleted, with the skin on (ensure that the pieces are about 3 inches by 6 inches in diameter, as this will help with even cooking)

½ cups (125 g) dark brown sugar

8 cups (2 l) water

1. First, brine the salmon. Combine all of the brining ingredients (the soy sauce, sugar, salt, garlic, ginger, and water) into a large bowl.

2. Place the fillets in the bowl and pour the mixture over the fillets. Cover the bowl and leave it in the fridge for around 8-12 hours.

3. The next day, remove the fillets from the brine. Pat the fish dry with paper towels.

4. Arrange the salmon on a cooking rack and leave it at room temperature for an hour.

5. Preheat the smoker to around 190°F (90°C) and add your pre-soaked alder wood to the loading tube.

6. Smoke for around 12 hours. The internal temperature of the fish should be around 130°F (55°C).

7. Serve the salmon alongside a tossed salad.

SMOKED OCTOPUS

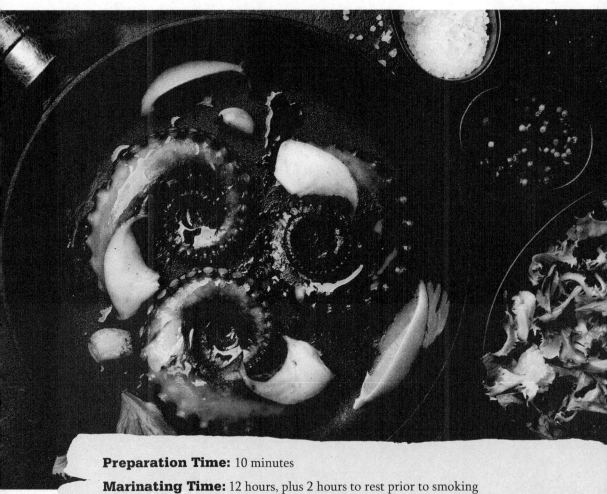

Preparation Time: 10 minutes

Marinating Time: 12 hours, plus 2 hours to rest prior to smoking

Cooking Time: 6 hours

Serves: 6-7

Preferred Wood: Apple or hickory

Nutrition Guidelines (per serving)

Calories 455; Total Fat 3.6g; Saturated Fat 0g; Cholesterol 0mg; Sodium 6mg; Total Carbohydrate 47.8g; Dietary Fiber 0g; Total Sugars 42.3g; Protein 55.1g, Vitamin D 0mcg, Calcium 48mg, Iron 1mg, Potassium 146mg

5 lb. (2 kg) fresh octopus, cleaned
1 cup (250 g) coarse kosher salt
1½ (500 g) cups maple syrup
4 cups (1 l) of water

1. Cut the octopus up into manageable pieces (around 170g / 6 oz. each). Make sure the pieces are roughly the same size so that they smoke evenly.

2. Brine the octopus. Incorporate the syrup, water, and salt inside a large plastic Ziploc bag or container. Add the octopus pieces to the bag and make sure that each piece is covered. Place the container in the fridge and leave it for about 12 hours or overnight.

3. Allow the octopus to rest for around 2 hours (no more) at room temperature to develop skin or glaze. This will enable it to hold the smoke once it is inside the smoker.

4. When it is time to smoke, preheat the smoker to around 120°F (50°C) to begin with. Place the apple wood chips inside the loading tube.

5. Smoke the octopus for about 2 hours initially.

6. Then raise the temperature of the smoker to around 150°F (65°C) and smoke for another 2 hours.

7. Finally, raise the temperature of the smoker to around 190°F (90°C) and maintain this for another 2 hours or until the internal temperature of the octopus reads 150°F (65°C).

SAUCY SMOKED SCALLOPS

Preparation Time: 5 minutes

Marinating Time: not necessary in this recipe

Cooking Time: 35 minutes

Serves: 6

Preferred Wood: Alder

Nutrition Guidelines (per serving)

Calories 187; Total Fat 5.6g; Saturated Fat 0.7g; Cholesterol 55mg; Sodium 268mg; Total Carbohydrate 3.8g; Dietary Fiber 0g; Total Sugars 0g; Protein 28g, Vitamin D 0mcg, Calcium 40mg, Iron 0mg, Potassium 537mg

2 cloves garlic, peeled and minced

2 Tbsp. freshly ground black pepper

2 lb. (1 kg) of high-quality sea scallops (20 scallops make one pound approximately)

Juice of 1 lemon

2 Tbsp. olive oil

1 Tbsp. coarse kosher salt

1. Preheat the smoker to around 225^0F (110^0C) and add the pre-soaked alder wood chips to the loading tube. Add one cup of water to the drip tray.

2. Rinse the scallops and pat them dry with a paper towel.

3. Incorporate lemon juice, olive oil, salt, pepper, and garlic together in a bowl.

4. Add the scallops to the mixture and toss well.

5. Place the scallops directly on a cooking rack, evenly spaced apart, so they do not touch each other, and smoke them for around 35 minutes or until the internal temperature of the scallops is around 125^0F (50^0C).

PERFECT PECAN SMOKED TROUT

Preparation Time: about 25 minutes

Marinating Time: 4-24 hours

Cooking Time: 2-3 hours

Serves: 6

Preferred Wood: Pecan

Nutrition Guidelines (per serving)

Calories 660; Total Fat 23.4g; Saturated Fat 0.1g; Cholesterol 0mg; Sodium 3mg; Total Carbohydrate 2.6g; Dietary Fiber 0g; Total Sugars 2.6g; Protein 102.8g, Vitamin D 0mcg, Calcium 3mg, Iron 0mg, Potassium 16mg

For the marinade:

¼ tsp. cayenne pepper

¼ cup lemon juice

½ tsp. salt

2 Tbsp. vegetable oil

⅓ cup dark brown sugar

1½ cups water

For the fish:

4-6 trout 1 lb. (1/2 kg) each

For the brine:

1 cup (250 g) coarse kosher salt

½ cup (125 g) light brown sugar

8 cups (2 l) of water

1. Combine the brine ingredients in a saucepan and heat over medium heat until the ingredients have dissolved. Allow the mixture to cool.

2. Place the trout in a flat dish and pour the brine mixture over the top.

3. Cover the dish with plastic wrap and place in the fridge for at least 4, but no more than 24 hours.

4. Prepare the marinade. Combine sugar, salt, lemon juice, oil, salt, and cayenne pepper.

5. Once the fish are finished brining, pat dry with a paper towel.

6. Pour the marinade over the top of the fish and place it in the fridge for a further two hours.

7. Before cooking, preheat the smoker to around 200⁰F (95⁰C) and add the pecan wood chips to the loading tube.

8. Remove the dish from the fridge and remove the fish from the marinade.

9. Smoke the fish for around 2-3 hours, or until the internal temperature is at around 145⁰F (65⁰C).

CORN
ON THE COB

Preparation Time: 2 hours

Marinating Time: not necessary in this recipe

Cooking Time: 1½ hours

Serves: 6

Preferred Wood: Apple

Nutrition Guidelines (per serving)

Calories 314; Total Fat 18.4g; Saturated Fat 4.1g; Cholesterol 10mg; Sodium 27mg; Total Carbohydrate 32g; Dietary Fiber 2g; Total Sugars 8g; Protein 4g, Vitamin D 3mcg, Calcium 1mg, Iron 0mg, Potassium 1mg

6 large ears of corn with the husks still on
6 Tbsp. olive oil
Salt and pepper for seasoning
Butter

1. Peel back the husks of corn but leave them attached to the cob. Soak the ears of corn in water for several hours.

2. Pat them dry with paper towels and lightly brush with olive oil.

3. Season the corn liberally with salt and pepper.

4. Preheat the smoker to 225°F (110°C) and add the apple wood chips to the loading tube.

5. Smoke the corn for about 1½ hours and serve with butter.

JALAPENO POPPERS WITH BACON

Preparation Time: 10 minutes

Marinating Time: not necessary in this recipe

Cooking Time: 1½ hours

Serves: 20

Preferred Wood: Hickory

Nutrition Guidelines (per serving)

Calories 77; Total Fat 5.1g; Saturated Fat 2.5g; Cholesterol 15mg; Sodium 198mg; Total Carbohydrate 1.6g; Dietary Fiber 0.6g; Total Sugars 0.6g; Protein 5.5g, Vitamin D 1mcg, Calcium 53mg, Iron 0mg, Potassium 60mg

10 medium-sized jalapeno peppers, sliced lengthways with the seeds removed

4 oz. (100 g) whipped cream cheese

4 oz. (100 g) cheddar cheese

4 slices of thinly cut bacon

1. Preheat the smoker to around 250^0F (120^0C) and add the hickory wood chips to the loading tube.

2. Place the bacon on a flat tray and smoke it for around 1 hour or until slightly crisp.

3. Coarsely chop the bacon and add it to a bowl, along with the cream cheese and the cheddar cheese. Place the mixture (1 tablespoon) inside each of the poppers.

4. Arrange the pepper halves on a tray and place them in the smoker.

5. Smoke for around 30 minutes.

GRILLED SMOKY EGGPLANT

Preparation Time: 20 minutes

Marinating Time: 30 minutes

Cooking Time: 40 minutes to an hour

Serves: 4

Preferred Wood: Apple

Nutrition Guidelines (per serving)

Calories 55; Total Fat 1.5g; Saturated Fat 0.2g; Cholesterol 0mg; Sodium 4mg; Total Carbohydrate 10.6g; Dietary Fiber 6.3g; Total Sugars 5.3g; Protein 1.8g, Vitamin D 0mcg, Calcium 16mg, Iron 0mg, Potassium 408mg

1 large eggplant

1 tsp. canola oil

1 tsp. smoked paprika

2 tsp. ground cumin

2 tsp. ground coriander

½ tsp. coarse sea salt

½ tsp. garlic powder

½ tsp. cayenne pepper

1. Preheat the smoker to 200°F (95°C) and add your hickory wood chips to the loading tube.

2. Cut the eggplant lengthwise or into ¼ inch (6 mm) thick slices.

3. Combine the oil and spice mixture in a large bowl. Add the eggplant slices to the bowl, coating them with the mixture.

4. Lay the eggplant slices on a flat tray and place them in the smoker on the cooking racks. Smoke for around 40 minutes.

SPICY AND SWEET NUTS

Preparation Time: 15 minutes

Marinating Time: not necessary in this recipe

Cooking Time: 45 minutes

Serves: 8-10

Preferred Wood:

Nutrition Guidelines (per serving)

Calories 318; Total Fat 32g; Saturated Fat 3.2g; Cholesterol 0mg; Sodium 80mg; Total Carbohydrate 7.6g; Dietary Fiber 4.8g; Total Sugars 2.8g; Protein 4.8g, Vitamin D 0mcg, Calcium 33mg, Iron 1mg, Potassium 188mg

For the rub:

½ Tbsp. chipotle seasoning

1 Tbsp. freshly ground black pepper

1 Tbsp. dark brown sugar

1½ tsp. sea salt

1 Tbsp. smoked paprika

½ tsp. ground cumin powder

3 cups (450 g) of any nuts of your choosing (but pecans are a good nut because they smoke well)

1. Preheat the smoker to around 250⁰F (120⁰C) and add your choice of woods, hickory, or cherry.

2. Soak the nuts for around 10 minutes.

3. Incorporate the rub ingredients together in a bowl.

4. Add the nuts to the bowl and stir well. Place the nuts on a flat baking tray.

5. Place the tray in the smoker and smoke for around 40 minutes. The nuts should be slightly browned.

PECAN SMOKED CHEDDAR CHEESE

Preparation Time: 30 minutes

Marinating Time: not necessary in this recipe

Cooking Time: 4 hours

Serves: 8

Preferred Wood: 4 hours

Nutrition Guidelines (per serving)

Calories 97; Total Fat 3.9g; Saturated Fat 2.4g; Cholesterol 12mg; Sodium 344mg; Total Carbohydrate 1.1g; Dietary Fiber 0g; Total Sugars 0.3g; Protein 13.7g, Vitamin D 0mcg, Calcium 233mg, Iron 0mg, Potassium 37mg

1 lb. (450 g) of white cheddar cut into 2 even sections

1. Preheat the smoker to around 90^{0}F (32^{0}C) in order to prevent the cheese from melting or exuding its oil inside the smoker. Add the pecan wood to the loading tube.

2. Place the cheese on the cooking rack directly and smoke for 4 hours.

SMOKED ICE CREAM

Preparation Time: 5 minutes

Marinating Time: not necessary in this recipe

Cooking Time: 10 minutes

Serves: 6

Preferred Wood: any wood will work here

Nutrition Guidelines (per serving)

Calories 137; Total Fat 7g; Saturated Fat 4.5g; Cholesterol 29mg; Sodium 53mg; Total Carbohydrate 16g; Dietary Fiber 0.5g; Total Sugars 14g; Protein 2.3g, Vitamin D 0mcg, Calcium 80mg, Iron 0mg, Potassium 131mg

4 cups (600 g) vanilla ice cream (or any flavor you choose)

1. Place the ice cream in a bowl and set it over a larger, flame-proof bowl filled about halfway with ice. Put the bowls in the freezer to rest.

2. Preheat the smoker to around 150°F (65°C). In this case, you want to create smoke, not heat. Add your wood of choice.

3. Smoke the ice cream (inside the bowls) on one side on the grill for around 5 minutes. You will see smoke start to rise from it lightly. Flip the frozen ice cream over and repeat the process for the other side. If it starts to melt, take it out. You can refreeze the ice cream to get it back into its shape.

DECADENT SMOKED CHERRY COBBLER

Preparation Time: 15 minutes

Cooking Time: 1 hour

Serves: 6

Preferred Wood: Cherry

Nutrition Guidelines (per serving)

Calories 484; Total Fat 8.3g; Saturated Fat 5.1g; Cholesterol 22mg; Sodium 153mg; Total Carbohydrate 99.2g; Dietary Fiber 2.7g; Total Sugars 74.4g; Protein 2.9g, Vitamin D 5mcg, Calcium 57mg, Iron 1mg, Potassium 100mg

¼ tsp. salt

1 cup (130 g) all-purpose flour

½ cup (125 ml) milk

¾ tsp. baking powder

¾ cup (180 g) sugar

4 Tbsp. butter

½ tsp. cinnamon powder

2 cans (1200 g) pre-prepared cherry pie filling

1. Preheat the smoker to around 250⁰F (120⁰C) and add your cherry wood chips to the loading tube.

2. Combine the flour, sugar, salt, baking powder, and cinnamon.

3. Add the melted butter and milk to the dry ingredients. Rub together until it forms a stiff paste or dough.

4. Pour the cans of pie filling into a greased cast-iron skillet.

5. Crumble the dough mixture over the top of the cherry mixture and finish with a light dusting of cinnamon or your preferred topping.

6. Smoke for 60 minutes and serve with ice cream.

BBQ
MOP SAUCE

Preparation Time: 10 minutes

Cooking Time: 10 minutes

Makes: around 5 cups

Nutrition Guidelines (per serving)

Calories 123; Total Fat 0.1g; Saturated Fat 0g; Cholesterol 0mg; Sodium 11mg; Total Carbohydrate 22.5g; Dietary Fiber 0.2g; Total Sugars 20.9g; Protein 0.1g, Vitamin D 0mcg, Calcium 17mg, Iron 1mg, Potassium 170mg

4½ cups (1.1 l) apple cider vinegar

1 tsp. salt

½ tsp. cayenne pepper

½ tsp. red pepper flakes

½ cup (125 g) light brown sugar

1 tsp. freshly ground black pepper

1. Combine the ingredients in a saucepan over medium heat. Add ¾ cup (180 g) of water to the mix as well. Stir gently until all of the ingredients have dissolved.

2. Use a small "mop" to apply the sauce to your favorite meats before smoking.

COLA MARINADE

Preparation Time: 10 minutes

Cooking Time: not necessary in this recipe

Nutrition Guidelines (per serving)

Calories 941; Total Fat 60.4g; Saturated Fat 7.8g; Cholesterol 0mg; Sodium 7875mg; Total Carbohydrate 95g; Dietary Fiber 1.5g; Total Sugars 82g; Protein 9.4g, Vitamin D 0mcg, Calcium 74mg, Iron 3mg, Potassium 422mg

2 cups (500 g) cola
½ tsp. fresh black pepper
Juice of 1 lemon
½ cup (125 ml) soy sauce
4 Tbsp. Worcestershire sauce
2 Tbsp. brown sugar
¼ cup (60 g) vegetable oil
4 cloves garlic crushed
1 tsp. sea salt

1. Combine all the ingredients in a large bowl. Apply to whatever meat you choose and leave to stand for about 8 hours or overnight.

SMOKED TEA RUB

Preparation Time: 5 minutes

2 Tbsp. Oolong Tea or Lapsang Souchong
1 Tbsp. ground espresso beans
1 Tbsp. crushed peppercorns
1½ tsp. onion powder
1½ tsp. garlic powder
1½ tsp. sea salt

1. Combine all the ingredients in an airtight bag and mix them thoroughly. Store for up to 3 months and use as necessary when smoking your meat, fish, or poultry.

FROM THE AUTHOR

Dear Friends,

I am glad to greet you on the pages of my cookbook **completely devoted to Sous Vide cooking**. Last year was very rich in events and meetings, but fortunately, my lifestyle has not changed, and I am still doing what I love most!

I enjoy spending a lot of time in the kitchen, **experimenting with new tastes, and verifying successful combinations**. And when choosing the meals, I most certainly keep true to my central principle: simple instructions and available ingredients. I am not writing exclusive recipes for master chefs — **I want *everyone* to enjoy them!**

This book is full of very different recipes! At first glance, they may even seem too different for the book-cover, but they all have one common feature — being vacuum-cooked at low temperatures.

Here I have collected my favorite and most successful recipes.

May you and your families enjoy these delicious tastes!

OUR RECOMMENDATIONS

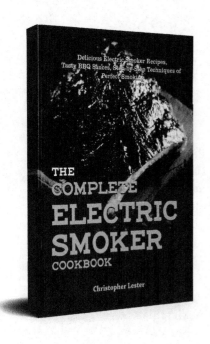

Complete Electric Smoker Cookbook: Delicious Electric Smoker Recipes, Tasty BBQ Sauces, Step-by-Step Techniques for Perfect Smoking

RECIPE INDEX

Thank you, Dear Readers!

I am so grateful for those who make up the community of readers that I love to write recipe books for! Thank you for your shares, encouraging emails, feedback, and reviews. I appreciate each one more than you, guys, know!

Copyright

ALL ©COPYRIGHTS RESERVED 2021 by Christopher Lester

All Rights Reserved. No part of this publication or the information in it may be quoted from or reproduced in any form by means such as printing, scanning, photocopying, or otherwise without prior written permission of the copyright holder.

Disclaimer and Terms of Use: Effort has been made to ensure that the information in this book is accurate and complete; however, the author and the publisher do not warrant the accuracy of the information, text, or graphics contained within the book due to the rapidly changing nature of science, research, known and unknown facts, and the internet. The author and the publisher do not hold any responsibility for errors, omissions, or contrary interpretation of the subject matter herein. This book is presented solely for motivational and informational purposes only.